Little People, **BIG DREAMS™**

KING CHARLES

Written by
Maria Isabel Sánchez Vegara

Illustrated by
Matt Hunt

Frances Lincoln
Children's Books

When little Charles Philip Arthur George was born,
the bells at Westminster Abbey rang out for a royal birth.
He was the first son of the future Queen of the United
Kingdom, which meant he would one day be king.

His mother became queen when he was three,
and he was named Prince of Wales six years later.

While his parents were busy with their royal duties,
the queen's mother gave him all the hugs he needed.
She also encouraged his love for art, music, and nature.

His father was a practical man who wanted his son to stand on his own two feet, so he sent him to a boarding school where the future king could rub shoulders with other boys. Far from home, Charles felt quite alone.

Things got better when Charles decided to go to college. He studied history and became the first royal to earn a degree.

In his spare time, he explored his artistic side, performing in plays and concerts.

Hoping to be a good prince for the Welsh, Charles spent some time studying at a college in Wales. He wanted to learn about its people and its language. But many were not happy with his visit, and he was met by furious protestors.

To get away from the attention, Charles took long walks into the mountains. All alone, surrounded by meadows, trees, and sheep, he was no longer the English-born prince but just a young man falling in love with Wales.

He promised himself to always do his best to protect those beautiful landscapes and the whole natural world.

Charles was twenty-one when he gave his first speech defending the environment, long before global warming became a well-known issue.

After completing his duty serving in the Royal Navy,
he used his final pay check to create a charity that
helps young people to fulfil their dreams.

The time came for Charles to find a wife to share his royal duties with. The day he got married, millions of people worldwide watched the ceremony on television. Lady Diana, his bride, looked like a fairy-tale princess.

But the couple had very little in common and ended up separating. Sadly, Diana died one year after their divorce, leaving a deep hole in the hearts of their two sons, William and Harry, and of the whole world.

When Charles married Camilla, his closest friend for thirty-five years, they bought a farm in Wales, far from any palace.

There, he planted trees, talked to his plants, and ate organic food, inspiring others to live in harmony with nature, too.

UN CLIMATE CHANGE CONFERENCE

Charles worked on hundreds of good causes that needed his support. He brought governments and companies together to protect the environment and urged world leaders to do better to preserve our planet.

As his mother grew older, Prince Charles took over more of her duties, from making speeches and meeting important visitors to traveling overseas.

Charles was a seventy-three-year-old grandfather when the queen passed away and he became king.

From then on, he promised to serve his people with love and respect, just as he had done since he was a child. It had been a long journey for little Charles, and after a lifetime of preparing for the job, he hoped not to let anyone down.

KING CHARLES

(Born 1948)

1951   1968

Charles Philip Arthur George was born at Buckingham Palace in London on November 14, 1948. He was the eldest son of Queen Elizabeth II (then Princess Elizabeth) and Prince Philip, Duke of Edinburgh. When King George VI died in 1952, Elizabeth became Queen of the United Kingdom, making three-year-old Charles the heir to the throne. He spent his early childhood at Buckingham Palace with his younger sister, Anne, but was sent to boarding school a week before his eighth birthday. Later, he joined his father's old school in Scotland, Gordonstoun, where he spent five years. After graduating from Cambridge University, Charles followed the family tradition of serving in the armed forces, training as a jet and helicopter pilot. In 1981, he married Lady Diana Spencer and the couple had two

1999

2022

sons together before divorcing in 1996. He married his long-standing friend Camilla Parker Bowles nine years later. On September 8, 2022, the Prince of Wales—the longest-serving heir in British history—became King Charles III following the death of his mother. During his time as Prince of Wales, he founded many charities, including The Prince's Trust, which helps vulnerable young people to get jobs, education, and training. He has always been a passionate defender of the environment, warning the world about the dangers of climate change long before it was widely recognized as a global issue. A champion of conservation, his philosophy is that to create a sustainable future, we must all live in balance with the natural world.

Want to find out more?

Have a read of this great book:

It's Up to Us: A Children's Terra Carta for Nature, People, and Planet
by HRH King Charles III and Christopher Lloyd

Text © 2023 Maria Isabel Sánchez Vegara. Illustrations © 2023 Matt Hunt
Original idea of the series by Maria Isabel Sánchez Vegara, published by Alba Editorial, S.L.U
"Little People, BIG DREAMS" and "Pequeña & Grande" are trademarks of
Alba Editorial S.L.U. and/or Beautifool Couple S.L.
First Published in the USA in 2023 by Frances Lincoln Children's Books, an imprint of The Quarto Group.
100 Cummings Center, Suite 265D, Beverly, MA 01915, USA. T +1 978-282-95900 **www.Quarto.com**

This book is not authorized, licensed, or approved by HRH King Charles III.
Any faults are the publisher's who will be happy to rectify for future printings.
A CIP record for this book is available from the Library of Congress.
ISBN 978-0-7112-8669-6
Set in Futura BT.

Published by Peter Marley • Designed by Sasha Moxon
Edited by Lucy Menzies, Claire Saunders, and Molly Mead
Production by Nikki Ingram

Manufactured in Guangdong, China CC022023
1 3 5 7 9 8 6 4 2

Photographic acknowledgements (pages 28-29, from left to right): 1. Princess Elizabeth with her son, Prince Charles, on the grounds of Clarence House, their residence in London, on August 9, 1951. © Alpha Historica / Norman James via Alamy Stock Photo. 2. Prince Charles learning to fly at RAF Tangmere in August 1968 in a de Havilland Chipmunk a single engined two seater trainer. © David Cole via Alamy Stock Photo. 3. PRINCE CHARLES IN A MEADOW OF WILD FLOWERS NEAR OAKSEY WILTSHIRE UK JUNE 2 1999. © Adrian Sherratt via Alamy Stock Photo. 4. Britain's King Charles III and Camilla, Queen Consort, greet wellwishers as they arrive at Hillsborough Castle in Belfast on September 13, 2022 © Niall Carson/POOL/AFP via Getty Images.

Collect the Little People, BIG DREAMS™ series:

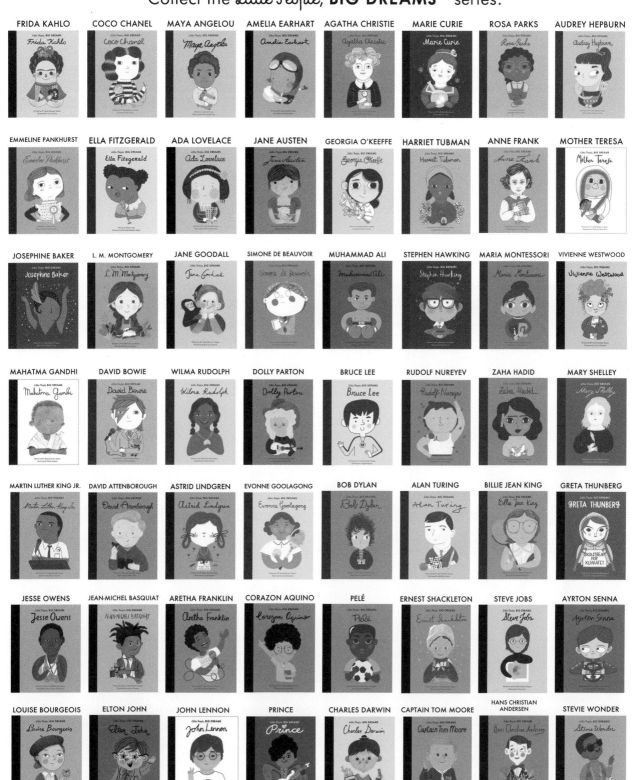

FRIDA KAHLO	COCO CHANEL	MAYA ANGELOU	AMELIA EARHART	AGATHA CHRISTIE	MARIE CURIE	ROSA PARKS	AUDREY HEPBURN
EMMELINE PANKHURST	ELLA FITZGERALD	ADA LOVELACE	JANE AUSTEN	GEORGIA O'KEEFFE	HARRIET TUBMAN	ANNE FRANK	MOTHER TERESA
JOSEPHINE BAKER	L. M. MONTGOMERY	JANE GOODALL	SIMONE DE BEAUVOIR	MUHAMMAD ALI	STEPHEN HAWKING	MARIA MONTESSORI	VIVIENNE WESTWOOD
MAHATMA GANDHI	DAVID BOWIE	WILMA RUDOLPH	DOLLY PARTON	BRUCE LEE	RUDOLF NUREYEV	ZAHA HADID	MARY SHELLEY
MARTIN LUTHER KING JR.	DAVID ATTENBOROUGH	ASTRID LINDGREN	EVONNE GOOLAGONG	BOB DYLAN	ALAN TURING	BILLIE JEAN KING	GRETA THUNBERG
JESSE OWENS	JEAN-MICHEL BASQUIAT	ARETHA FRANKLIN	CORAZON AQUINO	PELÉ	ERNEST SHACKLETON	STEVE JOBS	AYRTON SENNA
LOUISE BOURGEOIS	ELTON JOHN	JOHN LENNON	PRINCE	CHARLES DARWIN	CAPTAIN TOM MOORE	HANS CHRISTIAN ANDERSEN	STEVIE WONDER

Scan the QR code for free activity sheets, teachers' notes and more information about the series at www.littlepeoplebigdreams.com